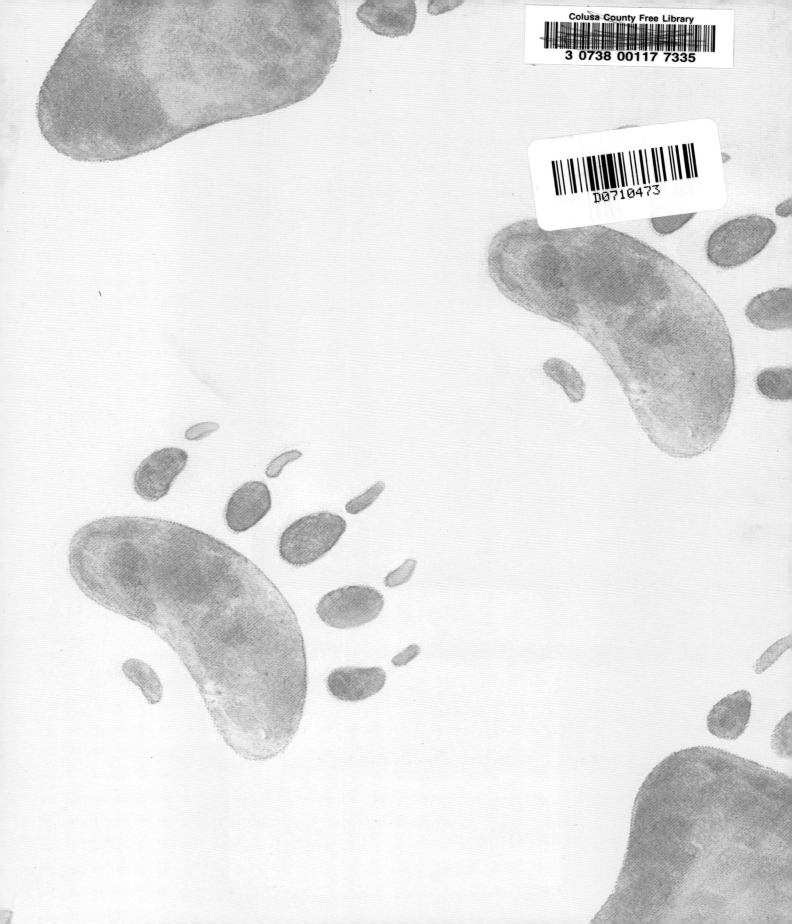

Two Bears There
The Story of Ahpun and Oreo

Written and Illustrated
by Dianne Barske

PO Box 221974 Anchorage, Alaska 99522-1974

Book Design by: Denise Martin

Library of Congress Control Number: 2003100090

ISBN 1-888125-49-7

Printed in China

This book is dedicated to John Seawell, zoo volunteer extraordinaire, who worked so hard to make sure the Alaska Zoo provided the best possible home for this unique pair — "the two bears there."

John Seawell with his model for snow leopards' enclosure (*photo by D. Barske, 2002*)

Introduction

Ahpun and Oreo came to the Alaska Zoo as orphaned cubs in the spring of 1998. Ahpun, the polar bear whose name means "snow" in Inupiaq, arrived first, in March from Point Lay. Children there had given her that name. One month later, she was joined by brown bear cub, Oreo, when she was orphaned at Mt. Susitna and brought to the zoo. A little girl, watching her play, noticed the white collar of fur around Oreo's neck, typically found on baby brown bears, and called out, "See, she looks just like an Oreo cookie, brown with white in the middle!"

Both bears needed a home and caretakers since they were without their mothers. Then there was the need for a playmate since they would normally grow up wrestling with their sibling cubs. The Alaska Zoo was able to provide these things for the bear pair, although at first it was questioned if the two would get along. In the wild, the brown and white bears might have been enemies, but as the months passed at the zoo, it became clear that these two were inseparable buddies.

Photo by 4th grade class of Laura Lappies, Hermon Hutchens Elementary School, Valdez, AK (2002)

The only time they were apart was "moving day," a day in July of 1999 when they were taken separately up the hill to their new large enclosure, complete with climbing rocks, waterfalls, and a deep swimming pool. Until they were once again side by side, they bellowed and bawled.

Now, years later and fully grown, Ahpun and Oreo remain constant companions — different from each other, true — still best friends, for sure!

There are two bears there —
one brown
and one white.

How can that be?

One should live on Arctic ice —
The other by tundra and trees.

But there are two bears there —
One polar and one brown.
How can that be?

    One eats rivers' fish and plants,

The other hunts seals from the sea.

Yes — but there are two bears there!
Living together at the zoo.

Both lost their mothers.
Now they've become family — these two.

"But this cannot last," some people say.

"This cannot be. A brown and a polar?

"Why, in the wilds they'd be fierce enemies."

But as orphaned
   cubs they came
To the Alaska Zoo,
They only knew
   each other as
   playmates,
These buddies,
   these two.

Without their
   mothers
They look to
   each other.

And the
   kind people
   at the zoo
Take care
   of these two.

The brown
  is called
    Oreo,
Like the
    dark cookie
    we know.

The white
  bear's
  Ahpun,
The Eskimo
  word for
  snow.

These two springtime cubs
How they love to play!

Swat! Trounce! Go wrestle!
Their play fills each day.

They play —
  Follow the leader
    Snatch the bear popsicle
      Catch the salmon
        Hide and seek
          Catch me if you can
            Bounce the bucket
              Queen of the hill.

In warm springtime sun
They cuddle and nuzzle.

But what will happen in winter?
That's a big puzzle.

Polar bears prowl through winter
But the browns go to sleep.
It's called hibernation,
The browns' deep winter sleep.

Will there not be
two bears there
Through long
winter's night?

Will Ahpun
be alone
As Oreo sleeps
out of sight?

But wait!
It's now turned to winter.
Is Oreo awake?
There are still two bears there!
They swat, pounce and shake.

As long as Oreo has her food
And a good friend in her sight
She'll roll in the snow — she'll snort
  and she'll snuffle.
All covered with snow, she too looks
  quite white.

As snows melt away
And a new spring's begun
The bear pair's much bigger
Now they're yearlings — age one.

They still tug and tussle.
They still charge and chase.
But their play's much more cramped.
They'll need much more space.

So what have we here?
Bears gone with no trace?

No — there are two bears over there —
Moved to a much bigger space.

There's a pool for deep swimming
Some rocks to explore.
Water streaming like rivers
New dens, space galore!

But will big bears stay friends?
No one seems to know.
Polar and brown stay best buddies
As older they grow?

Four years now
  have passed
Since the cubs
  first did meet.

There are two
  big bears there —
Big paws,
  great big feet!

Their swats are now bigger,
Their wrestling's more strong.

But — what do you know?
They still get along!

Yes — there are still two bears there.
Even when they grumble,
They lope and they lumber
Play tag, swim, and tumble.

Hooray for these buddies,
These two different bears.

They show us best friends
Can come in odd pairs!

Yes — THERE ARE TWO BEARS THERE!
A happy bear sight.

Oreo's
chocolate brown,
Ahpun's
snowy white.

About the author

Dianne Barske, artist and author, has lived in Anchorage for 28 years. She wrote and illustrated Mukluks for Annabelle, *published by the Alaska Zoo. Annabelle was the zoo's elephant artist and first resident animal. That book went on to win a national first prize for nonfiction books from the National Federation of Press Women in 2000.*

Dianne teaches art to children and finds that a great adventure. She is the mother of two sons and a daughter, and grandmother of two. Husband Elliott is a meteorologist. "He likes watching weather — I like watching people and animals," she states. "Watching Ahpun and Oreo together is about as fascinating as it gets!"

Paws and Claws *(The Bear Facts)*

Oreo and Ahpun are two very different bears. Oreo is brown and Ahpun is white! Oreo is a grizzly bear. Ahpun is a polar bear. Even their feet are very different. You can learn a lot just by looking at their paws and claws!

Ahpun's paws, especially the front ones, are big and wide. She uses them as webbed paddles for swimming. She might even shovel snow with them. Like all polar bears, she has fur between the pads on her feet to give her traction on the ice, and help keep her from skidding. Her foot fur is white, just like the rest of her fur. Polar bears' white fur makes them camouflaged on ice and snow to help them sneak up on the seals they eat for food in the Arctic. Ahpun's claws are shorter than Oreo's.

Brown bears' longer claws help them dig for food. They like to dig for plants, roots, and berries in the forest or on the tundra. Those long claws help them grab for a bug or a fish in a river. When Oreo was a little grizzly bear, she might have used those long claws to scamper up a tree. In the wild, her brown fur would help her blend in with the tundra or the forest's earth and trees.

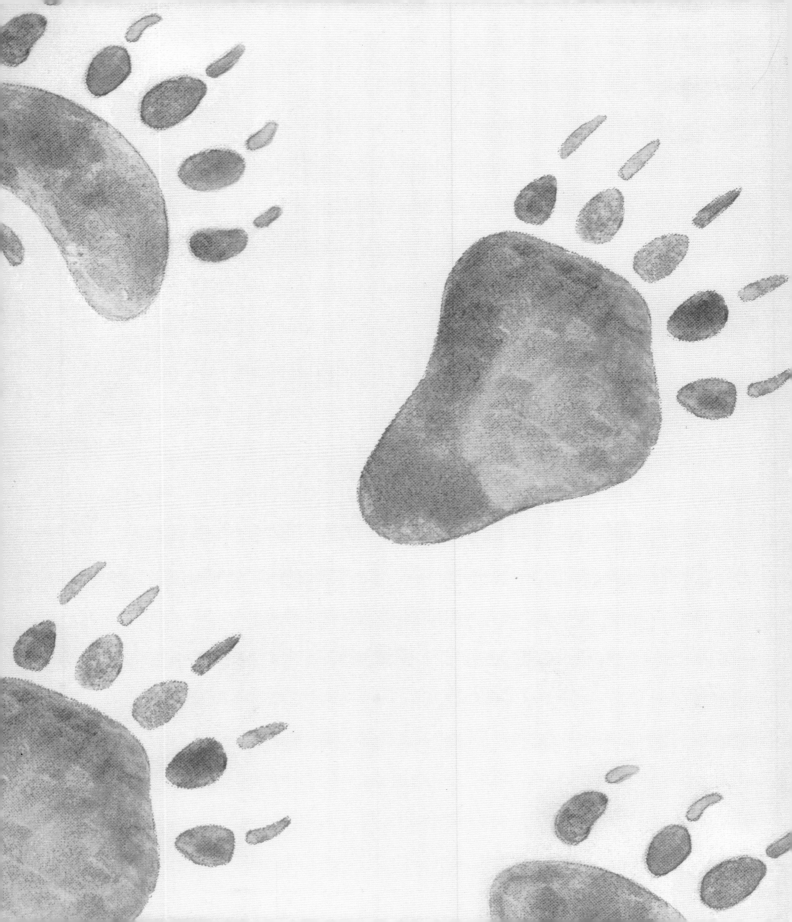